T0078394

My
Life's
Recollections

JAMES DONALD ETHERIDGE

WESTBOW
PRESS®
A DIVISION OF THOMAS NELSON
& ZONDERVAN

WestBow Press books may be ordered through booksellers or by contacting:

WestBow Press
A Division of Thomas Nelson & Zondervan
1663 Liberty Drive
Bloomington, IN 47403
www.westbowpress.com
844-714-3454

ISBN: 978-1-6642-7008-4 (sc)
ISBN: 978-1-6642-7009-1 (hc)
ISBN: 978-1-6642-7010-7 (e)

Library of Congress Control Number: 2022911567

Print information available on the last page.

WestBow Press rev. date: 07/20/2022

CONTENTS

CHAPTER 1

Growing Up Poor in the South

A life worth living is a life worth recording.

—Jim Rohn

The motive or reason for compiling a written documentation of my life is not that I believe history would desire it, but rather that I personally have a need to fill a void in my own life. My own parents did not leave any kind of written legacy, and I have always been curious about their lives. In the event my own children would desire a written record of my life, I thought it important to document what I remember. I have always tried to keep my mind active because I fully realize the consequences of not doing so. It is for these reasons that I am writing a record of my life.

I was born in a Miami, Florida hospital in 1936, the only one of my family not born in Alabama. During the 1930s, the country was in the middle of the Great Depression, and my father was in the Miami area working in a fruit-packing plant.

From my memories of early childhood, which took place during World War II, I remember my father teaching me to tie my shoelaces and parching peanuts on a woodstove. My mother and aunt were usually at the movies. The earliest recollection I have of early childhood is of crawling on the floor while my twin sisters were ironing, each with her own little ironing board. A neighbor stopped by our house and commented on how cute the twins were.

My father was a quiet man, slow to anger. He was well respected by his peers. I noticed this when I accompanied him. People called him "Mister" and listened attentively when he spoke. When I was seven years old, my father developed a serious condition that we were told was the effect of a brain hemorrhage. While working in Florida, he was robbed and knocked unconscious. This injury caused a clot to form in his brain, from which he later died.

I knew my father was a Freemason because, when he died, the Masons provided his funeral. He wore a Masonic ring, which I remember had the builder's square and compasses and the letter G in the middle. The Masons were very clannish then, and remain so even to this day. I once worked at a place where, to be eligible for advancement, you had to be a member of this organization. Even now, the thought of a college sorority bothers me. Respect should be earned by merit and hard work, not by membership in some organization.

The fondest memories of my father were when he hid Easter eggs in the lumberyard for us kids to hunt. I also remember him and my uncle making home brew, which my mother objected to. She attended the Baptist church on Sundays. I have no knowledge of my father ever being drunk.

We lived in a three-room house furnished by the lumber mill where my father worked. Our groceries were purchased from the store owned by the lumber mill. The lighting consisted of a single bulb hanging from the ceiling. A wood-burning stove located in the center of the living room provided heat. This stove would glow red and orange.

I would become frightened when my mother and father argued, which was mostly about money. My mother was about having a good time, and my father was serious about balancing the budget. We were still in the Depression, and our lives were affected by this.

I remember an event when I was five or six. We had been discussing my father's passive attitude and decided to provoke him to anger. There was a watermelon wrapped in a blanket with ice to cool, which I rolled off the porch. My father's reaction was to give me a single blow with the back of his hand on my rear.

I do remember my father's reaction when my sister Jeanette told him that a girl named Nora dropped off the mail. He

3

misunderstood, thinking she was speaking of a Black man with a similar name. He went into a rage because he thought a Black man had handled his mail. This was the only evidence of his bigotry I ever witnessed.

I had twin sisters, Jean and Jeanette, who my father referred to as "the twins." He was very protective of them. I remember an occasion when he thought a strange man had threatened them. He grabbed an ax from the woodpile and charged down the road to confront the individual. I do not know or recall what happened next.

My family consisted of two brothers and two sisters. We went through the usual sibling rivalry. I remember fishing in a little pond close to our house in my brother's favorite spot. He had been attempting to catch a large fish for months, which I was lucky enough to catch.

When I was about seven years old and learning to read, I remember irritating my older brother by following him around the house and yard while reading from schoolbooks. He was constantly terrifying me by covering me with a bedsheet. This was probably the root cause of my claustrophobia.

My older brother was of the adventurous type, and was always my hero. He wanted to join the Merchant Marines. The government was paying huge salaries because the casualty rate was extremely high. German U-boats were sinking our ships when we shipped supplies to Russia and England, who were fighting the Germans. I attempted to follow in his footsteps by joining the paratroops while in the army years later. I never could match him physically, so this did not end well.

My little brother, Thomas, was breastfed, and I remember my mother putting a burning substance on her breast to discourage my little brother from feeding.

When my father died, my mother was left with a tremendous burden. She was left to care for five children, ages four to thirteen. It seemed that the kitchen was always dirty, with unwashed dishes in the sink and ants crawling all over the counter. The sugar was always covered with ants and not usable. When I lived at home, it was a waiting game to eat. My mother had a pressure cooker, and we had to wait until the beans would cook. I remember once taking the pressure regulator off before the steam was released and being burned.

The financial assistance my mother received was eighteen dollars for each child per month. This represented my father's social security. After my older brother entered the military, he sent an allotment each month to my mother.

We lived next door to a Ford dealership, and the manager would give Thomas fifteen cents each week as a reward for keeping out of the facilities and allowing the workers to work. Thomas would buy candy and cookies, which he would share with me.

The owner of the Ford dealership was a bald, overweight little man who was deathly afraid of his wife. My mother would ask me to take a note to him requesting a temporary loan, usually five dollars. He would give me the money but would always say something about his wife or what she might think. It was almost hilarious to watch him grimacing. I was about ten years old then.

CHAPTER 2

Living in Monroeville, Alabama

The small city where I spent my early childhood was Monroeville, Alabama, which was also the county seat. The town was centered on a city square where the city hall and police station stood. The county sheriff was my mother's first cousin. He must have weighed around six hundred pounds.

We would all go to Limestone Creek, the local swimming hole, and swim. I could not swim myself, so my older brother, John, taught me. He did this by throwing me into the creek, where I learned to swim in a hurry.

My little brother and I would seldom go to school; instead, we would gather pecans anywhere we could find them. They were easy to sell, and we would use the money to buy toys. One day, after we had each bought cap pistols and holsters, we began shooting the guns off at home. At that moment, the truant officer was inside listening to my mother explain that the reason we were not in school was that we were sick.

Around 1946, Thomas and I walked through the door of the local Western Auto store where we were met by the owner. He told us to look around and select anything in the store as a Christmas gift. He must have realized that we would not have Christmas unless someone else provided. It was probably the way we were dressed. We were probably dirty and looked underprivileged. I was struck by the compassion that this man showed to people he did not know and had no personal relationship with. He had just seen us in the neighborhood and thought that we needed a Christmas gift.

One day, my little brother and I were out riding our bicycles, and I noticed my friend Melvin sitting on his front porch with his mother and father. I was about nine and my brother was about six. We both let go of the handlebars and stood upright with our feet planted on our seats. We did this, of course, to show off in front of him and his parents. I have never seen anyone do this trick before, and I find it hard to believe even to this day.

Around the fourth grade, I confronted death and realized its effect on people. During this time, one of my school friends lost his mother to cancer. When he returned to school after the funeral, his mood was somewhat different, and I did not know to how to cope with this. After several weeks, he came around and was his old self, much to my delight.

On the first of the month, my mother would receive her social security check. She would always go to the store and purchase chocolate milk and Moon Pies. I constantly waited for the first of the month.

My mother had a live-in boyfriend, and one day the welfare lady came by the house. She was shocked to see my mother lying on her boyfriend's bed. My mother explained that this was her boarder's bed, but the welfare lady was still shocked. It was not long after this that my siblings and me were relocated to a foster home.

I was approximately ten or eleven years old at the time. My older brother, John Amos, ask me to accompany him on a mission. He had discovered that the fence around the Western Auto store was loose, and he needed a lookout so he could go into the store. I watched for a while, but became frightened at the prospect of being caught. I ran home and left my brother unprotected. My brother came home with all kinds of goodies from the Western Auto store. It was then that I realized that I might be a coward, or at least less than daring.

When I was about twelve years old, my mother arranged for me to assist one of her friends, Bernard, who worked one of those traveling photo booths. We went all over Alabama and worked the Fourth of July crowds. Barnard would take the photos and I would develop them. This gave me a chance to work with science for the first time and I really enjoyed myself. We were making photos at a Fourth of July picnic with an all-Black crowd. One of the women wanted a not-so-nice picture of herself. She kept insisting, and Barnard snapped it. He came to the booth where I was developing the pictures and told me to fix the solution so the photo would not come out. He explained that should we develop the picture, we would end up in jail. This was my first experience with not-so-nice women.

We live in Monroeville, Alabama after my father's death. The city was on a city square with most businesses and the courthouse within that square. My little brother and I played within this area most of our young lives while living with our mother. One day, a kid passed by and began to curse us both. We told him to control his mouth, or we would clobber him. He continued to curse us. I knocked him around a bit, but he would not stop cursing us. I realized then that I was not prone to violence and could not beat anyone up. I realized that I had no stomach for it. We turned the kid loose and told him to go home to his mother.

From where we lived, it was only about two blocks to the elementary school. I remember hearing the fire siren and, naturally, I needed to investigate. While the firemen were dragging their hoses along the ground, I thought it might be fun to place my bare foot against the moving hose. This resulted in an exceptionally large sore on my right foot. I never came to understand why I would do such a foolish thing, but I did.

My sister, Jeanette, worked in the local theater as a ticket taker. My brother Thomas and I would be allowed admission when she was on duty, provided the manager was not looking. One day when I sat down in the theater seat, I sat on a bag containing a lady's dress. I thought the dress might fit my mother, so I took it home with me. Someone must have seen me with the bag because I was questioned and confessed. When I returned the dress, they barred me from the theater for a little while.

We lived about four blocks from the theater and after watching scary movies, I would run down the middle of the street until I reached home. It was too scary to walk down the sidewalk because of the trees with their overhanging branches. This was where the werewolves and cat people would hide at night.

My brothers and sisters and I were employed to sweep out the theater after the movies were over. There was always uneaten popcorn left in bags, which we ate. There were also coins, which spilled from customers' pockets, on the floor and in the seats, which we recovered while sweeping.

The house where we lived behind the Ford place must have been repossessed, because we ended up living about four miles out in the country. I remember one winter when it was freezing cold, we broke up the furniture and burned it in the heater to keep warm. I do not remember being hungry for an extended period. Waiting for the beans to cook was the only time I have a recollection of that.

One day, both of my sisters and I were walking into town to

work at the theater, about four miles away. It began to rain, and we all went for shelter inside a storage shed filled with peanut hay. After eating raw peanuts for a couple of hours, I fell asleep. I saw evidence that rats had been eating the peanuts, and I realized that the rats could have been eating me while I slept. The weather suddenly changed from hot to a refreshing cool. I often think of this time and wonder if the danger of being eaten by rats, or the refreshing weather change, was the cause of this remembrance.

CHAPTER 3

Harder Times after Father Dies

World War II and rationing I remember very vividly. Sugar rationing was the one that most affected me. My aunt would send me to the store with a rationing book once each month for our ration of sugar. We used the sugar to sweeten our Kool-Aid and blackberry pies.

There was an incident when I was in the second grade that I remember very well. I needed to use the bathroom, but our teacher would not allow this during class. I managed to poop in my pants, which was noticed by the teacher and the other students. I believe the teacher suspected me because she asked if I had been sick. The ride home on the school bus was very embarrassing for me because all the students moved away from me during the ride home.

When I was in the third or fourth grade, I was sent home from school because I hit one of my playmates with a brick. This kid was a bully and he pushed me out of line just to be mean. My mother was forced to apologize to my teacher before I was allowed readmission.

After my father died, I remember going to the doctor for medication due to a tapeworm. He told my mother not to allow me to eat anything greasy. In those days, they packed sausage with grease in cans. I managed to eat several of these. When my mother found out, she became terribly upset and called my uncle Leslie. He assured her that I would be all right, which I was, of course.

My mother used part of my father's death insurance to purchase a home for us. We lived behind the Ford dealership in a small house with no electric power or inside bathroom. There were hundreds of abandoned cars with kudzu plants covering them. We had a billy goat who would slip up on us and butt us off the parked cars. My brother Thomas and I would play in the woods by our house for countless hours of fun. We used homemade rifles constructed out of wood and discarded inner tubes from old cars. We called the rifles rock guns.

At one point, I decided to wire our house with electric lights. I accomplished this by removing discarded batteries, wiring, and headlights from old cars. The only problem was that the batteries would only last for about one night.

The reason I spent so much time at my Aunt Ida Mae's house was because her boys were approximately my own age. During one period when I visited overnight, there was a terrible hurricane. The trees in front of my aunt's house were destroyed, but her house was not damaged. I remember she threw a mattress over me and my cousins to protect us.

After the death of my father in 1943, I spent a lot of time at my aunt's house. One which I recall is when my cousin ran off with a neighbor's daughter and her father paid us a visit riding bareback on an old mule. He wanted his daughter back. His daughter and Clyde went to my uncle, who was a preacher, and he married them.

When I lived with my Aunt Ida Mae, my cousins and I would pick wild blackberries, place them in a jar, cover the jar with a cloth, and allow fermentation to occur. After waiting for about a month, we would drink the wine which developed.

At one point in my life, I lived with my aunt Ida Mae who had five sons in the military. One of the boys turned out to be a real war hero. I do not remember the exact details, but he ended up being awarded the Silver Star, and a silver plate was inserted in his skull due to an injury.

My Aunt Ida Mae's house was next to a small creek where people occasionally gathered to gamble, in defiance of local law enforcement. One very cold morning I awoke to see a Black man struggling to keep warm, next to my aunt's wood-burning heater. I had never seen a Black man this close, and I was naturally curious. At this point in life, I was about ten years old. Finally, my aunt confronted me because of my staring. She explained that she observed the individual freezing in the outside cold and invited him to come in to get warm. This person was gambling with several people and was apparently winning when they decided to rob him. They knocked him out and left him for dead. My aunt prepared breakfast for everyone including the Black man. This was the first time I had observed any kind of compassion by a white person for a person of color in the segregated South.

During the period when I lived with my Aunt Ida Mae, her son Leonard returned from service in the U.S. Army. He took off a money belt with $26,000 and laid it on her bed. When his mother asked where he got the money, his answer was that he had taken it off dead German soldiers. He increased this amount by gambling on the boat going home. Leonard decided to invest his money with a half interest in a sawmill. Some of his competitors burned down his sawmill and he lost all his investment.

One day, I was playing in some tall weeds, and I cut my ankle on a piece of glass. Leonard placed me in his new car, and on the way to the doctor's office, I bled on his seat covers.

My aunt had a Black maid named Louise, who was pleasantly plump. She would grab me from behind and squeeze me. I remember she had a long scar on her cheek where she said her husband had cut her.

One of my other cousins deserted the army during basic training. The military police knocked on my aunt's door looking for him. He hid from the MPs in the local graveyard, but they caught him just the same. Desertion during wartime is a profoundly serious offense, but he only served six months in the stockade.

After watching a Tarzan movie at the theater, I decided to make a spear out of a long tree branch. To do this, it was necessary to cut the branch, which I did with the aid of my aunt's kitchen knife. I placed the branch on a railroad track and hit it with her knife, which immediately broke. My aunt was upset with me for breaking her knife. One of her boys overheard her complaining. He took me aside, gave me money, and told me to buy her a new knife, saying I had found the money in a paper sack.

CHAPTER 4

Living Away from Home in Foster Care

In about 1947, I was sent to live with my Aunt Callie Dalky. She lived in the north Alabama town of Cullman. What I remember most about her was her stability. She was a retired schoolteacher with a firm grip on life.

My aunt had a tenant living in her rental house on the same property. This tenant had a small child who was watching her father cut wood one day. A wood splinter rebounded into her eye and the mother was beside herself. My aunt calmly reassured the young lady that the child would be all right, which she was. I gained a new respect for my aunt because of the way she handled this situation.

There was a grape vineyard located on the property, which my aunt and uncle used to make wine and grape jelly. I could eat grapes whenever I desired.

My Uncle Andy Dalky was an immigrant from Germany and a former soldier. He fought on the side of Germany during World War I. He believed that children should only listen and speak only when spoken to. He was not a bad person; he was only strict.

My cousin Doris was a teenager at this time. She had a friend living across the street who tried to teach me to play softball, but with little success.

I remember the whole family, including me, picking cotton. The thing that is most memorable is when I picked in a sunny area of the field and went into a shaded area. This was the most wonderful feeling in the world. With the money I made picking cotton, my aunt bought me a new suit, which I wore home on the train back to my mother's house.

The entire family went to a Catholic church every Sunday, but the entire service was conducted in Latin. I had no idea what the priest was saying, but I have always regarded the Catholics as very interesting.

In one incident, my cousin Doris came home from school and related a story of a man dragging his dog down the street with a rope tied around the dog's neck. My aunt found the man and lectured him for half an hour about cruelty to animals.

The reason I was sent home involved my cousin David. He wrote bad words on the sidewalk, which his mother saw. He blamed the whole thing on me, but I was innocent. Maybe his mother thought I was a bad influence.

Much later, both David and Doris were schoolteachers at the local school. David was the principal. One of my relatives told me that, before his death, David went blind.

During my period of staying in foster homes, I attended a school, which consisted of one room with grades first thru sixth. My teacher was an exceptionally large woman named Mrs. English. Some of the kids dared me to kiss a blond-headed girl, and Mrs. English spanked me with a baseball bat cut in half.

While living with my foster parents, we would attend a Holiness church on Sunday. The members of the church would speak in weird languages, jump over seats, and make strange sounds. After the service, the members would turn on their lights and, on one occasion, they witnessed two of my classmates being inappropriate in the grass. The girl quit school because of the embarrassment, and the boy instantly became the school hero.

It was about the sixth grade when I attended Castleberry Elementary in Castleberry Alabama. I remember the red clay and the smell of pine trees. At recess, some of us boys would play mumble the peg with our pocketknives. One of the girls would always play with us. She was either a tomboy or enjoyed playing with us boys rather than with girls. She was tall and slim with blond hair.

When I was about twelve years old, I was sent to an orphanage in Jasper, Alabama. I am not sure where my other siblings were then. I know that my older brother, John Amos, was in the army and overseas, stationed in Guam. The orphanage had about sixty children, both boys and girls. This was the only period in my life where I experienced any stability. Everything was institutionalized. Everyone ate and slept as instructed. The girls were upstairs and the boys were downstairs. Everything was, of course, very neat. We were required to keep our sleeping quarters in proper order and were not allowed to lie on our beds during the daytime.

We had recreational areas with a basketball goal out front. I would practice basketball for hours. This is where I would conduct my social activity. Some of the girls from the school would come by and talk to me. This one girl would write me notes, make a statement, and give me the option of checking yes or no at the bottom. I heard a country and western song recently with the same title, "Check Yes or No." For some weird reason, I was quite popular at this school. I believe I was a novelty here because I lived at the home. Maybe it was because my previous school was a lot harder than this new school, and I did a lot better academically here.

The director at this orphanage was also the local Scout master, and he allowed me to complete the Boy Scout test when I wanted to. The Boy Scouts were a good experience for me. I learned a lot and it also built up my self-esteem. Probably the worst thing about the home was that we were forced to eat foods that we did not like. They had a storage building outside where they stored canned goods that people donated. Some of the other boys and I found a way to enter and when we were hungry, we would eat what we wanted.

I remained at this facility probably for a little less than one year, until my cousin Dorothy and her husband rescued me.

CHAPTER 5

Cousin Dorothy Rescues Me

Dorothy and Shelton Morgan visited the orphanage in Eldridge, Alabama and asked me if I wanted to go home with them on a trial basis. I said yes, of course I would like to leave that place. I heard that Shelton had a traumatic experience in the army while awaiting shipment, pending invasion of the Japanese islands. It was said that he had cracked up on board ship. I never noticed any unusual behavior while I was living with him. He was discharged from the army on a general discharge and awarded a disability for life, so he probably had some problems.

Dorothy was a loving and caring person, and the only relative I knew who finished high school. She helped me make health posters for show and tell at school. The letters were cut out of colored paper and glued to poster board. She chose the most colorful vegetables in the magazines that were available at this time. I always received outstanding grades for my posters.

Dorothy and Shelton had a baby girl, Linda. I loved her dearly; she was so soft and cute, and I spent a lot of time playing with her. At this time, they were building their own home, and everything was purchased individually, as the money became available. There was an incident where my mother's husband objected to me living with Dorothy and Shelton. I cannot recall the details, but I remember Shelton was upset and it almost came to blows between the two men.

My brother Thomas L. lived with my Aunt Clara at the same time I lived with Dorothy, who was, of course, her daughter. I remember one incident when my little brother was upset, and my Aunt Clara was petting him. I wanted some attention for myself, so I pretended to cry. My aunt saw through this immediately and she scolded me.

There was one occasion when my aunt did come to my aid. I was delivering the local paper to her neighbor Mrs. Ward, and I asked to collect the monthly fee. The neighbor did not appreciate my collection approach and began scolding me. My aunt overheard the conversation and tore into this woman on my behalf.

Sometime later, we moved back in with our mother. She and her second husband had gotten a divorce, and she was now working at the hotel coffee shop in Demopolis, Alabama. One of my mother's customers was a laundry delivery man, named J.D. Lovett. He mentioned that he needed someone to assist him in delivering the laundry. At this point, I was probably about thirteen years old, and I was excited about working and making money. We began our route delivery and immediately became great friends, discussing the various houses we delivered to. As we approached one house, which was constructed out of logs on the exterior, I made the comment, "I'll bet a Black person lives here."

He replied, "No, this is where I live." The reason we stopped was that he wanted to eat breakfast. He fixed a nice breakfast for both of us, and we continued our work. The house he lived in was genuinely nice; just the outside was made of logs.

When I was in the ninth grade, I had a bicycle which was made to deliver groceries. It had a huge basket in the front with a ridiculously small wheel touching the ground. One day, several friends and I decided to see how many of us could ride this bicycle at once. We were probably encouraged by the college fad of seeing how many students could fit in a telephone booth. Our teacher, Edwina Wilson, happened to drive by at this time and witnessed our attempt. She told the class what she had observed during class the next day.

One of my high school friends was a boy named Billy Briney. He was large for his age and when we played football, I would follow him through the line with him blocking. It was rumored that when he was born, he weighed sixteen pounds. We were inseparable for my entire school experience, and we remained friends for life. I heard that he had died back in the seventies.

My ninth-grade teacher was Edwina Wilson, who we all

were very fond of. She was fresh out of college and this was her first teaching assignment. All of us kids would cut up in her class because she was like a special friend to all of us. After some time, we decided to cool it for fear we would get her in trouble. Once Edwina was sick and five or six of my friends and I took flowers to her in the hospital. She was one of the few teachers that I still remember in a positive manner.

I considered it my duty to talk and clown around in class, which would result in my being thrown out of class. We had a football coach named Chink Lott who would check the halls; if he saw anyone standing outside, he would take you to the bathroom and hit you with a baseball bat split down the middle.

I had an English teacher named Barnes who is the object of many of my fond memories in high school. She was obsessed with restoring an old rock house at our school. She asked for volunteers to help her in the reconstruction of the rock house, but she received little help from any of my fellow students. My fellow students and I made fun of her when she quoted Shakespeare. I suppose it was the unique way she enunciated each passage. Of course, we did this behind her back, but I believe she really knew we were poking fun at her.

James at 14 or 15 years

One of my next-door neighbors was a boy named Jimmy Wallace. His father was a well-dressed, professional looking man. I met his mother and his autistic sister. You could tell that his family accepted the little girl's condition and treated her normally. I remember trying to not notice her sickness, and everything went very well. Jimmy and I were great friends until we had an encounter involving my dog Baby. We were at the river and Jimmy thought it a good idea to throw my dog into the river. When I saw him do this, I immediately slugged him. Jimmy was a little larger and in better physical condition, so he got the better of me. I was upset by this and refused to associate with him for several weeks. Eventually, though, we resumed our friendship and when his father was transferred to another state, we parted as friends.

One night, several friends, including Jimmy, and I thought it might be fun to spend the night in a graveyard. There were about five of us boys in our group and we each had our own .22 rifle. We settled down for the night next to some of the tombstones. Everyone went to sleep except me; I was too scared. I kept hearing noises. Finally, I heard a noise in one of the trees and I promptly fired a couple of shots into it. Everyone asked what I was shooting at, and I explained that I thought there was a cougar in the tree. From that night on, my nickname became Cougar.

One of the most colorful characters I associated with during my early years was physically attractive, a nice dresser, but had the morals of a tom cat. I first met Andrew at his car lot. I was employed to take payments from his customers when he was away from the lot. This allowed me the opportunity to learn to drive by lining up the cars on the lot. Andrew had his hand in several ventures, such as selling watermelon and fish from booths located in the surrounding towns. The fish he sold were mostly carp and buffalo, which his crews caught from the two rivers bordering Demopolis, Alabama.

Once, Andrew sent me to Florida with his truck and driver to purchase a load of watermelons. This was profitable because the watermelons would ripen first in Florida and were easy to sell in Alabama. On this trip, I overpaid for the load of melons, the driver got drunk, wrecked the truck, burst the watermelons, and was arrested. I had to call Andrew to come get me and he was not extremely impressed with my day's activity.

CHAPTER 6

Bigotry

I witnessed one of the most shameful eras in American history. I refer to the plight of Blacks in 1950s Alabama. One day, a young Black man and his attractive wife came by the car lot searching for a car. There were two bad men there who started harassing the young black man. They used the term "boy" numerous times, and made sexually suggestive remarks to the man's wife. They invited the man and his wife to go with them to an isolated place. The man became noticeably enraged and told the men he would agree to meet them privately. His wife begged her husband to walk away from the encounter, knowing the consequences if her husband should attack the white men. The reality was that if a Black man struck a white man in early 1950s Alabama, he would have been hanged from the nearest tree without trial. This was the reality in the deep South. A Black person had no civil rights during this time.

My brother and I spent a lot of time at the city dump. We always had our air rifles with us. One day, we decided to start a war with some of the Black kids who were at the dump. We had a foxhole already dug, which we shot from. I raised up to shoot one of the kids, but he got me first in the left eye. My little brother Thomas charged the Black kids and shot some of them before they ran away.

I was driven to Selma, Alabama to see an eye doctor, but my sight returned before we arrived at his office. I wore sun glasses for several weeks following this, but I do not believe there was ever any permanent damage.

My closest friend in high school was Austin Cleveland Wright. We both lived in an apartment house by the river. There was a small house at the rear of our apartment which we converted into a club house. There were four members in this club: A.C. Wright, his brother Willy, me, and my brother Thomas L. About a block away was a large grocery store named Jitney Jungle. I was too chicken to participate, but the other members would steal candy from Jitney Jungle and bring it back to our club house to share.

A.C. was very athletic and he would be allowed to choose sides when we played football. Since I was a poor athlete, when other people would choose, I was always the last person chosen. When A.C. would choose, I was always chosen first. He wanted me on his team although he knew we would lose.

The primary recreational outlet when I was a small boy was

on the river. Demopolis, Alabama was bordered on two sides by rivers. There was an activity known as jump fishing, which we were engaged in one night. The object of this sport was to sneak along the banks of the river and punch under the rocks. This caused the fish to jump. They would either jump short of the boat, over the boat, or into the boat. Loaded into a small wooden boat was A.C. Wright, myself, A.C.'s father, and Ed Randal, who was the boyfriend of A.C.'s sister. One of the members punched under a rock with the boat paddle and an alligator gar jumped into the middle of our boat. With its many teeth, this thing looked like a real alligator. To make room for the gar in our boat, I immediately jumped into the water and swam to shore. One of the people in the boat attempted to kill the gar with the aid of the boat paddle. This activity resulted in knocking a hole in the boat, which promptly sank. All the occupants of the boat ended up in the water and were obliged to swim to shore, where I was already positioned. This became an amusing story to relate to our friends.

A.C. and I would swim in the river constantly. I suppose the reason we did this was because it was free. We would swim across from one county to another, which was about two hundred and fifty yards. We gave little thought to the dangers involved. There were extremely poisonous water moccasins, alligator gar, and other large fish. Even today, it is hard to believe we could do this without fear.

One day after swimming across the river, we noticed a small

boat motor lying on the ground. We thought it might be a great idea to tie the motor to a tree and throw it back into the river for safe keeping. I made the mistake of mentioning this to my next-door neighbor, and he in turn informed the chief of police. It seemed the motor belonged to a federal employee whose job it was to lower and raise the water flowing over the dam. My neighbor paid to have the motor dried out and repaired to keep us out of jail.

If you had a dime, you could swim all day at the Demopolis swimming pool. Some of my friends and I would swim at night when the pool was closed. When the police car came with its spotlight, we would crowd the back of the pool so the light would not detect us.

There were three towers you could dive from, but only the most daring would attempt a dive from the top. My little brother Thomas could do a perfect swan dive from the top. I noticed people watching him, mostly the girls. I thought I should share the attention, so I attempted a swan dive myself. The results did not go well, and I ended up in the hospital with weights holding my neck in place. The local doctor misread the X-rays and assumed I had a broken neck. What followed was weeks in the hospital and a body cast after I was released. The doctor wanted me to wear the body cast for several weeks, then be fitted with a neck brace. I decided not to comply with this. I cut the cast off my body, and never went back to the doctor. Later, when I entered the army, the doctors informed me that my neck had never been broken.

I saw my first dead man while living in our apartment house. One day, I heard a large noise. Lying in the muddy road was a man with half his face blown away, shot by another man who he argued with. The dead man had cut the other man on the side of his head, so the other man went home and got his shotgun. The last time I saw the man with the shotgun, he was sitting in the police car on the way to jail. I never knew what happened, but I always hoped he was released.

CHAPTER 7

Harder Times, and Feeling Disheartened

The summer of 1951 was a terrible time for me. We were forced to move from our apartment in the old Masonic home, to another town, way out in the country. At this point, I was isolated from all my former friends, and I felt completely demoralized. I believe we moved because of my sister. Her husband, Don Myers, was in the Air Force, and stationed at Craig Field in Selma Alabama. He had just been discharged and returned home to Ohio; my sister, of course, went with him. I believe he was paying the rent on our apartment at the Masonic home. After he and my sister left, we could not afford to live there anymore.

Not far from our house out in the country lived my uncle Howard Day, my mother's brother, who was a preacher. He was always impoverished and living in low-rent, run-down houses. I do not recall him ever having any material goods. To help and comfort other people was his only goal in life. My uncle's life contrasted with present day television ministers worth millions and even billions of dollars. We were visiting one Sunday and there was absolutely nothing to eat in the house. As always, I had my .22 rifle with me, so I went hunting for food. A rabbit jumped up in front of me and I took a shot, which drilled the rabbit through the head. This was one of the best meals I have ever eaten.

I managed to return to my former hometown of Demopolis for brief stays. My former neighbors, the Thomases, allowed me to sleep on their back porch. I was fed by my previous next-door neighbor. I still felt a warmth of friendship, which of course did not last. The saying that absence makes the heart grow fonder did not work in this case. Being absent allows people to forget about you.

In August of 1952, my mother decided to return us to Demopolis Alabama, because school would start in September. We managed to rent an apartment in an old wood frame house, which should have been torn down years before. What I remember most was the summer heat and the quest to get away from mosquitoes.

As I returned to school to start my tenth year, the atmosphere was quite different. Although it has been over sixty-four years, I can still sense the change. Some of my old friends had moved on to other interests. During my previous school years, I was completely obsessed with school—not with the academic part, but with the social part. I lived to attend school and to mingle with my friends. This part of my life was gone forever.

In October of 1952, I was involved in an incident which did not exactly endear me to some of my teachers. My best friend Wright was involved in an altercation with one of our teachers, a Mrs. Tally. She slapped A.C. and he slapped her back. She asked me to go get the principal and, of course, I refused. We both left the school, and when the principal caught up with us in his car, he told A.C. that he was expelled, and told me to walk home by myself.

In November of 1952, I was in class and suddenly decided to terminate my high school efforts. It was nothing that occurred on this day, just an accumulation of problems to that point. What made me decide to throw in the towel is still unclear to me. Part of the problem had to do with economics, because I could not compete socially with my classmates by wearing nice clothes and getting a haircut when needed. I was never part of the class elite, and never invited to parties or to watch TV in a home on the only TV set in town.

CHAPTER 8

Out with School, in with the Army

After leaving school, I had a lot of time to reflect on my life and to ponder what would happen in the future. I thought it was important to upgrade from high school dropout to prominent member of society. The way I chose to do this was by joining the United States Army. It is true that I was influenced by watching movies from World War II and the Korean War. The one thing that influenced me most was my brother, who was in the army and had seen service in Korea. I assumed that this was an opportunity to redeem myself from dropping out of high school.

After my decision to pursue a military career, some of my friends decided on a going-away party. I must admit that the number of people who attended was a surprise to me. The reason was probably that some people just like parties, but there were, I believe, some people who generally had an affection for me.

The party lasted for several hours, and I must admit it gave me an ego boost. I went to bed that night both pleased and excited about leaving for the army the next day.

In November 1952, I caught a ride with my cousin Doris's husband, Harold Smith. He dropped me off at the recruiting office in Selma, Alabama, which was about fifty-two miles from Demopolis. All of us recruits were put on a bus and driven to Maxwell Air Force Base in Montgomery Alabama. My first night was both exciting and scary. The thing I remember most was the extremely bright lights which they turned on in the morning. I awoke to a sergeant screaming, "Everybody up! On your feet!"

After we were fed, they took us to the flight line, and we boarded a private civilian airplane, which was equipped with a stewardess. Our destination was Columbia, South Carolina, home of Fort Jackson. This chartered airplane was probably built in the early 1930s. When we were flying, the rivets and bolts squeaked, and it sounded like the plane would fall apart. I sat next to the window and when I looked out, I thought the engines were on fire. The stewardess assured me that the plane was not burning up, and that the problem was exhaust heating up and spewing fire. They considered this to be normal. It seemed abnormal to me since this was my first time on a plane. In any event, we landed safely at Fort Jackson in South Carolina.

Fort Jackson was, in 1952, what was referred to as a replacement depot. It is important to remember that in 1952, we were in the middle of the Korean War and thousands were conscripted into the Armed Services. We were placed in ten-man tents with single light bulbs hanging from the ceilings for light, and vented heaters in the middle of the tents for heat. Most of the men who were in my tent were much older than I was. At sixteen, I was regarded as a celebrity because of my young age. I represented sons that some of the men who were drafted had left at home. I was well received by my tent mates. I took full advantage of my new but temporary status. The army presented each of us with a $20 bill, which most of us immediately spent at the post exchange. I do not remember seeing a $20 bill before that time, and I felt rich for a while.

Every morning after we returned from breakfast, we were assembled and informed where we would be sent for basic training. At this formation were hundreds of men who were sent all over the southern states for training. Some remained at Fort Jackson for infantry basic training.

One morning, they called out my name and the names of three other soldiers and informed us that we were going to Fort Campbell, Kentucky, which was the home of the 11th Airborne Division. From among the hundreds of others assembled came the words, "You will be sorry."

My obsession with the paratroops started with movies, radio, and newspaper articles about the heroic accomplishments of the airborne forces. I knew from the start that this was a unit I would join. My motivation was further influenced by interaction with my brother, who had served with the 11th Airborne in Japan. What I lacked were all the physical attributes. I weighed about 107 pounds at this time, was extremely skinny, and in no shape for this activity. What should have given me a wakeup call was when I went through the shot line, two of the medics remarked, "This is Airborne." I checked in with the 11th Airborne on the first of December 1952, but we soon learned that training would not start until January 1953.

I often wondered what had happened to all the weapons that were used during World War II. Since there were over eight million men at arms during the war, the number of weapons must have been massive. After I started basic training, this was no longer a mystery. I found that they were being issued to the new recruits. These weapons were packed in cosMoline, a heavy black grease used for preservation. My first job in the military was to get the cosmoline off my M1 rifle. The only way to do this was to submerge it in boiling water. The rifle had to be completely stripped down first.

CHAPTER 9

Basic Training Nightmare

In January of 1953, trouble broke loose when our training began. We all received new identities: we were now identified as meatballs, fools, and cruets. The Black NCOs called us cruets, short for recruits. A basic training group was in 1950s made up of the lowest form of being found on this planet. The New York and Chicago ghettoes and slums had opened their gates. This was war, and the army needed killers.

The training was designed to allow each recruit as little sleep as possible. Our day started at 3:30 in the morning, and lasted until dark. Regardless of how hard we worked, it was never good enough. We were being brainwashed to make us mentally tough, and I can still feel it to this day.

We marched for miles with heavy machine guns on our shoulders on the way to the machine gun range. I remember the weight of the gun pressed into my shoulder. I learned to project my mind and think of more pleasant things like music that I enjoyed, and pleasant memories of my old friends.

There were classes almost every day, and what contributed negatively was the freezing wait to get into the classrooms. To keep us awake, we were required to wear our helmet liners, which were made of plastic. The reason was to enable the cadre to hit us on the head with a leather club when we were caught sleeping. The only time I ever got more than five hours sleep was when I was in the hospital with pneumonia.

When they wanted to harass us, they would call for what was called a G.I. party. They would wake us up in the middle of the night and have us scrub the wooden floors, on our hand and knees, with a stiff brush. Of course, the floors were never clean enough, so we were required to do it again.

There were two incidents which I have always regarded as cruel. One of the recruits refused to shave, so he was held while in formation, and dry shaved in extremely cold weather. The other act of cruelty involved a recruit who did not like to shower. He was pushed into the shower and scrubbed with a stiff brush.

Each morning, we stood formation in a battalion size formation. Each company commander gave a status report regarding how many people were AWOL or present. One morning, Item company reported 107 men AWOL. This struck some of our recruits as amusing, and we made the mistake of laughing. This infuriated our trainers, so they ran us for two miles with weapons and field packs.

Once, one of the sergeants was thrown out of a black sedan by the main gate, suffering from a thorough working over. He sustained a broken leg and arm and multiple face injuries. It was rumored that he had mistreated a recruit who had mob connections. This recruit had alerted his mob friends in Chicago. The FBI were called in, but I never learned if the perpetrator or perpetrators were ever caught.

We were required to work in the kitchen, which the military call Kitchen Police, or KP. When this happened, it usually lasted for eighteen hours at a time. I was on KP only twice during my training and that was enough for me.

After a couple of months of having all this fun, I decided that maybe I should wait until I was little older to go through all this nonsense. I requested to speak to the company commander and explained that I was only sixteen and underage. He immediately talked me out of going home. My mother had signed a document swearing that I was seventeen. He said that he was not sure, but they could prosecute my mother if they wanted to, and in any event, I would probably be drafted later. Since I was already halfway through training, it might be easier to just go ahead and complete it. This sounded reasonable to me, so I stayed in.

We were standing in line waiting to go into the mess hall to eat breakfast when one of my fellow recruits, a kid named Gallatin, decided he did not like the way I combed my hair or something. He decided to take a poke at me. We slugged each other for a while, and I gave him a black eye and knocked him down, but he put a knot on the back of my neck. After I knocked him down, he got up and shook my hand because I had not kicked him while he was down. I was just hitting him because he was hitting me. Anyway, that was the only occasion where I was in a fistfight during my basic training.

My training sergeant was a Sergeant Newman. He did not like the way that I was wearing my helmet when I was in formation, so he told me to put it on backwards, which I did immediately. The company commander noticed this, and he told the sergeant to have me straighten up my helmet. The sergeant questioned this, and I heard the company commander say, "Sergeant, you heard what I said." This was a few days after I talked to the company commander about resigning. That conversation could have influenced his attitude, but I do not know for sure.

I had done something wrong. I cannot remember exactly what that was, but one of the corporals assigned me the task of cleaning the outside of the barracks with a toothbrush. I took a bar of soap and went outside. I was cleaning the outside of the barracks when an officer came by and laughed. He asked me if I was going to do the entire barracks and I told him that was what I was told to do. Someone came for me shortly because I had a class or something that I had been assigned to, and that was the end of my chore.

Another form of humiliation used a lot was to require a recruit to climb on top of the barracks flapping his arms and reciting, "I am a big bird and I have been goofing off." I do not remember how many times I had to do this; it was probably several. It seemed like somebody was always up there flapping his arms.

The infiltration course was one of our training requirements. This was comprised of an area of about 100 yards. There were two machine guns, which fired crisscross eighteen inches over our heads. We crawled through mud and briar patches. The night that I went through, it was raining and I kept getting the barrel of my rifle clogged up with mud. When this happened, they forced me to go through again. I went through three times that night. I noticed that when the machine guns crossed, they fanned out. I took this opportunity to get up and run so I would not have to crawl.

They needed to teach us how to handle hand grenades, so they put us in a pit and gave us a live grenade. We would hold onto the handle and throw the grenade. A grenade cannot explode until after the handle flies off so there is really no danger if you have a firm grasp on the handle. One recruit froze up and could not release the hand grenade, so the sergeant took it from him and threw it. Something like that at sixteen was exciting to me and I never had any fear of anything they told me to do.

In another training exercise, we were inside a gas chamber with our gas masks on. There was tear gas everywhere and we were required to take our masks off and recite our serial numbers before leaving the chamber. I made the mistake of running out of the chamber. I was made to repeat the process.

The tear gas hurt your lungs and burned your neck. This was a very unpleasant experience.

There was an exercise where we dug a foxhole and a group of tanks would run over us. The tanks had an opening and one of the tank crew told me to crawl in. I thought this was cool at the time, but I would have second thoughts today.

About halfway through our sixteen weeks, we were sent out into the wilderness on a snow-covered ground in freezing weather. We stayed out for about a week, sleeping in two-man pup tents. I was in a tent with my friend Bob Jarmon. When you go through extreme hardship with someone, this makes you friends forever.

One day while out in the wilderness, my friend Bob Jarmon and I noticed a rope stretched across a river. The rope was probably about seventy-five yards across. I understood it was where the Army Rangers trained. Bob and I decided that we would try it. We slung our rifles on our backs and, carrying full field packs, we tried to walk across this river using our hands and the rope. Bob got about halfway across and dropped, and I dropped off right behind him. I could not hold on any longer and, of course, our rifles and our clothes were soaked. This was in the middle of winter and freezing cold. I think this was about the time that I went to the hospital with double pneumonia. The biggest problem was getting all that rust off my M1 rifle. It took months to do it because there are so many places rust can hide in a rifle.

One morning after we returned to a wooden barracks, I awoke with a burning fever. When we were in formation, the first sergeant called out sick call, and anyone who was sick had to fall out in front of the orderly room. He said this in a sarcastic voice. I immediately fell out of formation. He told me to quit complaining and get back in formation. I explained that I was sick, so he had a corporal run me all the way to the hospital, which was about a mile. When I was examined, it was determined that I had double pneumonia. I happened to overhear a conversation between my doctor and the first sergeant. The sergeant was threatened with court martial for having me run all the way to the hospital. I kept my distance from the first sergeant for the remainder of my training.

CHAPTER 10

Fort Benning, Here I Come

My stay in the hospital was very enjoyable for me; it was my best time during my entire training. I could sleep all I wanted and rest. I believe the length of my stay in the hospital was about ten days. Did I mention that as an army private, I was paid the enormous sum of $78 a month?

The end of basic training was bittersweet for me. During the past four months, all our activities had been planned, and we were on an extremely strict and organized schedule. It was unnecessary for us to think; thinking was done for us. It was almost like a feeling of being lost or confused. Instead of being told what to do, we were now asked, we had choices, and could decide for ourselves.

My platoon sergeant was now my friend. He called me aside and gave me encouragement for my future. He told me to keep a low profile at jump school and to never call attention to myself.

Until that time, I had never regarded Sergeant Newman as a human being. He was just someone who hollered at us.

There were always people around who wanted to make extra money. Two sergeants from another company agreed to give us a ride to Fort Benning for $20.00 each. Bob Jarmon and I only needed to go as far as Montgomery Alabama, because from there we went west to Demopolis.

Before we could leave, it was necessary to turn our rifles into the supply room. We attempted this several times and were always told that our rifles were dirty or rusty. The two sergeants went with us to the supply room and used their influence to get us checked out. At last, we could leave for home and leave Fort Campbell for good.

The two sergeants who were giving us a ride to Fort Benning were no ordinary soldiers. They were both Army Airborne Rangers, and I suppose you could say they were used to living life on the wild side. Along the interstate in Tennessee were many taverns where these sergeants would stop for a drink. I guess they were drinking beer. Bob would go in with them, but I would stay in the car because I did not drink. They kept doing this, and every time they would go in and come back, they seemed to be a little drunker. They were driving 100 miles an hour down the highway, and I was literally scared to death. Finally we reached, I believe, Gadsden, Alabama. The car that I was in was stopped, waiting on the light to change. In the car in front of us was an older woman. The car behind rammed us and propelled us into the rear of the vehicle the old lady was driving. Bob Jarmon was drunk and had vomited all over his uniform. While we were waiting for the police to show up, I pulled Bob from the car and took him into the Greyhound bus station. We sat by the window and watched the police arrest everyone in both cars.

I managed to clean Bob up and we caught the first bus to Demopolis by way of Montgomery. As we waited in the bus station in Montgomery, Alabama, we were approached by some former World War II paratroopers. They were disturbed because they thought we were kids dressed up in real paratrooper uniforms and we were trying to claim what they called "Dead Men's Glory." After some explaining that we were not wearing jump wings and were on leave prior to reporting for jump school, they were satisfied, and we parted as friends.

After we arrived in Demopolis to begin our ten-day leave, I immediately introduced Bob to all my friends. It is unclear to me why Bob went home with me rather than going to his home. Perhaps there were reasons he did not share with me. I was only glad to have him with me.

On my second day home, I went to my old high school, and entered my homeroom class. The principal told me to grab a chair and sit next to him. That began a session of show and tell. The whole class seemed interested in my adventure with the army. I was, for the first time in my life, the center of attention. As I found out later, the only person I was trying to impress was not impressed. She only said that I looked funny with my hair cut short. There was no mention of my sharp paratrooper uniform or the hardships I had gone through for the last four months.

My friend Bob was having the time of his life. He met a lot of girls in Demopolis. They thought Bob was a conquering hero. He was probably well received because he was a very handsome young man, and he was from another state. I believe Bob was from West Virginia.

After staying in Demopolis for ten days, it was time to board a bus for Fort Benning, Georgia to begin our jump school training. When I boarded a Greyhound bus in Demopolis, I noticed sitting in the back of the bus one of my Black friends who had gone through basic with me, a boy named Willy Evans. I went to the back of the bus and sat with Willy. When I did this, I noticed a lot of people staring at me. In those days, Black people had to ride in the back of the bus, and white people normally did not sit with them.

When the Greyhound bus crossed the Chattahoochee River, we were suddenly in Columbus, Georgia. There was another bus which took us to the main post at Fort Benning.

Fort Benning Georgia 1953

CHAPTER II

Life at Fort Benning, Georgia

I was assigned to barracks with most of my basic training friends. There were a group of soldiers from Hawaii who were thrown in with us.

The next morning, I was sweeping the floor by my bunk when one of the people from Hawaii asked to use my broom. I do not remember what I said, but I must have insulted his mother. He was an excessively big boy for his age, and he clobbered me good. Some of my friends picked me up off the floor. When I looked up, Willy Evans had lifted the boy off the floor and told him that there would be no more trouble, or the trouble would be with him. Willy was six-foot-seven and weighed around 240 pounds.

While we were training, we were required to wear a heavy jumper helmet with an itchy chin strap. The running I accomplished easily, but I had trouble with the physical training.

We were out in 100-degree, high humidity weather. They would stand us at attention and leave us there for five or ten minutes. People began to fall out one at a time.

One of the cadres was a large Cherokee who was about six-foot-six. A small corporal took a dislike to him for some reason. This little corporal gave us all a hard time, but especially the Cherokee. The corporal started screaming at the Cherokee and, before we realized what was happening, the Cherokee picked the corporal up and threw him into a nearby swimming pool. Of course, we all laughed, and this did not endear us to the other training NCOs They thought it would be a good idea to run us for a couple of miles in the Georgia heat.

We were joined in our training by members of the Air Force and Marines. The thirty-four-foot tower was our first objective. A person would go up a spiral staircase to the top and stand in the door of a mock aircraft. You were attached to two lines and, when you exited the door, you would fall about twenty feet. We were trained to grab the outside of our reserve chute while falling through the air. Somehow, I could never get it right. We were only required to make one correct exit. I jumped eighteen times in one day but never correctly. I would do a dead man's fall when I exited the door. There is some evidence that a sixteen year-old boy is prone to be awkward and I was no exception.

There was a way to quit having all this fun. You could refuse to jump, and you would be unhooked and dismissed from training. On one occasion while standing in front of me, seven men refused to jump. They were unhooked and immediately disqualified from training. One Air Force trainee, who I had become friends with, told me that he could see his ex-wife laughing at him when he stood in the door. I do not believe that any of the people who refused to jump were afraid—they just wanted out. I was too dumb to quit, and they had to throw me out.

When you were fully exhausted, they would give you a physical training test, which almost no one could pass. This included pushups, squat jumps, pull-ups, and other exercises. This was the method used to disqualify me. As I reflect, it was probably a mistake to go home for ten days and allow myself to get soft. Our training class started with three hundred men and only seventy graduated. I believe it was a matter of statistics. The paratroops only wanted a few to complete training and you needed to be almost superhuman to do this.

After flunking out of jump school, I was sent to a replacement company for processing to a permanent duty station. While waiting, I pulled Kitchen Police one day on and two days off. This was not a bad deal, not at all like basic training KP.

My orders came through in about a week. I was assigned to an infantry unit, the 30th Regimental Combat Team. Fort Benning was divided into three sections: Main Post, Sand Hill, and Harmony Church. My unit was at Sand Hill.

The purpose of this unit was to support the infantry school. We would put on demonstrations, like acting as a company in attack over difficult terrain. I remember one demonstration where we ran for about 200 yards to our first position. We had a muscular man we called Swede who carried a 57 recoilless rifle on his shoulder and jumped a ditch with the rifle still on his shoulder. He was absent one day for some reason and I took his place. When I attempted to jump the ditch, I fell in. I am not sure how heavy this rifle was, but I believe it weighed about thirty pounds. The thing that I am sure of is it was too much for me.

We were assaulting a position and I saw four soldiers disappear in a cloud of dust. They were firing 81-millimeter mortars over our heads, and one round fell short. These people were about 200 yards to my right when this happened. This makes you realize how vulnerable you are in a live fire exercise. It took some time for me to get over that and move on. A film crew were filming this exercise and I wondered if they kept the tape.

CHAPTER 12

Private First Class at Sixteen

Because I did not gamble or drink, there was little to occupy my time, so I concentrated on polishing my boots and brass. This was noticed by my superiors, and I was soon promoted to Private First Class. I remember sewing on my stripe and how immensely proud I was at the time. As I marched along, I kept looking at the single stripe sewn on my sleeve. I was seventeen years old and already a PFC in the United States Army.

Phoenix City, Alabama was just across the 14th Street bridge from Columbus, Georgia. Phoenix City was known in military circles as Sin City. If you walked down the middle of the street in Phoenix City, you could see the slot machines through the open windows. If you went inside one of the pawn shops, there would be a display of knives, brass knuckles, sawed-off shotguns, and other methods of destruction. Almost everything was considered illegal, but the police looked the other way.

One night, I went inside one of the bars and was approached by a pretty girl in a tight-fitting dress. She asked if I would buy her a drink and I immediately said yes. I learned later that she was drinking Kool-Aid and I was paying for liquor. In those days, the girls who worked in bars were known as B-Girls.

I drank minted gin while sitting at the bar. I thought I was unaffected until I stood up and realized my legs would not support me. That was when I realized it was time to exit Sin City. As I started to walk across the bridge, I heard glass breaking and looked back to see a solder lying in the middle of the street. He had been knocked through one of the plate-glass windows of the bar. At the same time, a military police car drove up with all four doors open. The MPs came out with guns drawn. The soldier who went sailing through the bar window picked himself up and ran past me on the bridge. One of the MPs pointed a 45 automatic pistol directly at me while telling the soldier to halt. While witnessing this activity, I thought it might be prudent to jump from the bridge into the river. While I was contemplating my next move, the soldier put his hands in the air and surrendered to the MP. His action prevented me from taking a cold dip in the Chattahoochee River. This was enough adventure for one night, so I walked across the bridge to the bus station and returned to camp.

I met Earlene Weaver, a middle-aged woman, who lived in an apartment complex just across the river in Phoenix City. She had two daughters who were still in high school. Her apartment became a second home for me, and I enjoyed eating Sunday dinner with her and her two daughters. I had no romantic interest in either daughter, but they took the place of my own sisters, who were, of course, elsewhere.

Earlene had been married to a prominent Baptist minister, who was pastor of a local church and who also wrote weekly articles for a local newspaper. I never asked why they were divorced. I suppose I was too embarrassed.

Earlene told me to make myself at home in her apartment and to go to her bedroom when I wanted to rest. One weekend, I opened the door to her bedroom—at the wrong time. This incident so embarrassed me that I did not return to her apartment for months.

In 1954, Albert Patterson, a local Phoenix City attorney, was elected to the office of Alabama Attorney General. His law office was about a block from the apartment of Earlene Weaver, where I was visiting one Sunday night. Earlene's daughters were on the couch talking to me about school and doing their homework when we heard a loud noise like a car backfiring. We learned the next day that Albert Patterson had been assassinated before he could take office. He had promised to clean up Sin City if he were elected.

The next weekend, when I attempted to enter Phoenix City, entrance was blocked by the Alabama National Guard. The Alabama governor had declared martial law. All military personnel from Fort Benning were prohibited from entering

Phoenix City. I continued to visit the city disguised as a Central High School student. I dressed myself in a white T-shirt, rolled up dungarees, and Ked tennis shoes.

Meanwhile, back at Fort Benning, this proud Private First Class continued to work as support for the infantry school. One of our jobs was to work with the machine gun committee, sitting at a table and pointing out nomenclature on a machine gun. We taught students from West Point, officer candidate school, ROTC, Korean officers, Vietnam officers, and others.

CHAPTER 13

Corporal Etheridge, Carl Beavers, and Betty

Eventually, I was noticed by a major who oversaw the machine gun committee. This major approached me and asked if I would like to be a permanent member of his committee. He explained that he was impressed with my attention to detail, shiny jump boots, and starched uniform. I, of course, immediately accepted his offer and was permanently assigned to his group. After working for a few months, I was promoted to a two-stripe corporal. I thought at this time that I was Jesus Christ.

One of the benefits of military service is an opportunity to interact with other people. There is a closeness brought on by continuous access to each other. In civilian life, you are with other people only eight hours a day, in contrast to twenty-four hours in the military. It was in this kind of atmosphere that I was privileged to know Carl Beavers.

Carl was a plain country boy with little formal education. He was full of homespun humor and extremely easy to talk to. We spent countless hours together as fellow members of the machine gun committee.

We were instructing a class of Korean officers on live fire exercises and the machine guns were deployed in line with the targets. Since the class was to continue the next day, the principal instructor directed Karl and I to watch the weapons overnight. It was during this all-night guard duty that I became close friends with Carl. We talked all night long, mostly about his wife Hattie, and his little girl Caroline. Karl mentioned that he had an old Dodge car that he wanted to sell. I needed a car, so I went to Carl's house a few days later to look at the car.

When I opened the door to Carl's apartment, there was sixteen year-old Betty Atkins, who was exceptionally pretty and the sister of Carl's wife. I had decided to purchase the car and before I left, I mentioned to Betty that I would be on CQ (Charge of Quarters) that night. I asked her to call me and, to my surprise, she did.

This began a period in my life when I spent all available time with Betty. We went to drive-in movies and spent a lot of time together at Carl and Hattie's apartment.

Finally, Betty returned home to Woodstock, Georgia, and I commuted every weekend that I was not on duty.

Young Betty at 15 years

One weekend on the way to see Betty, I gave a ride to a lady and her daughter who needed to go to north Georgia. We were on the outskirts of Noonan, Georgia, which was about fifty miles from Columbus, when my old Dodge ran out of gas. After buying a can of gas, I asked the young lady to hold the brake while I poured gas directly into the carburetor. She allowed the car to roll back, and the gas landed directly on a hot engine. Of course, the car began to burn. I put the fire out with sand, which went through the carburetor into the engine. The car never did run right after that. The girl and her mother caught a bus and continued their journey. I caught a ride the rest of the way to Woodstock.

I continued to commute between Columbus and Woodstock any way that I could. Finally, I bought another car, a 1947 Chevrolet and this made life a lot easier for me.

Once, after coming back from visiting Betty in Woodstock, I had had little sleep. The next day, when I attempted to drive through the main gate at Fort Benning, I ran the stop sign, with several military police officers watching. I was hauled before an officer, who took away my privilege to drive on base for thirty days. I was also forced to attend a mandatory driver's school. This restriction forced my mother to drive me to the bus station every day.

CHAPTER 14

Married at Eighteen

My mother and I rented a duplex apartment in Columbus, Georgia. It occurred to me that marriage would make my life a lot less complicated, so I asked Betty's mother and father if we could get married, and they agreed.

With her mother and father's blessing, my mother and I drove to Woodstock and collected Betty Jo. We all gathered at the Columbus, Georgia courthouse in search of a judge to marry us. I was able to prove that I was eighteen years old, so I did not need permission to marry. Betty was, on the other hand, only sixteen, so she needed her parents' permission. My mother was present at the wedding and the judge assumed that she was Betty's mother. I did not do anything to correct the judge on his assumption. The judge charged us five dollars for performing the ceremony. The thing I remember about our wedding was a remark the judge made. He told us to never get mad at the same time.

I had promised Betty's mother that I would venture back to Woodstock after we were married, And I kept my promise. We spent the night at her parents' house.

The day after our marriage, I decided to teach Betty how to shoot a rifle. I handed the rifle to her to set some bottles in a row to shoot at. While I was setting up the bottles, she accidentally fired off a round, missing me by a foot or two. She was almost a widow after being married only one day.

After one day of marriage, it was time to return to Columbus and Fort Benning. We had a one-day honeymoon with my mother and the next-door neighbor present in the living room. The next day, my mother drove me to the bus station, and I returned to Fort Benning to serve on my committee. I also had guard duty that night. I did not see my new wife until the following day.

After my one-day honeymoon followed by guard duty, my body was almost exhausted. We had a class of South Korean officers who were taking machine gun live fire exercises. I was responsible for about thirty of them while they were firing. As each student completed firing, I would ensure that the bolt of the machine gun was back and would insert a block in the receiver to render each gun safe.

Newly married Mr. & Mrs. James Donald Etheridge 1954

After my last student completed firing and all weapons were cleared in my area of responsibility, I would hold my arms up to show the principal instructor that it was safe for the students to go forward and check their targets.

In my exhausted state, I walked directly into a machine gun while it was still firing. One of the South Korean officers grabbed me by my shirt and pulled me back just in time. I remember him saying, "No Boy-a-san." This was the second time in as many days when I was almost killed. My married life was becoming dangerous.

When we were married for about two weeks, the company first sergeant asked to see me. He had in his hand an order to ship me to Alaska. I explained that I was recently married and did not desire to be shipped overseas. His reply was that

• James Donald Etheridge •

I belong to the United States Army, and they could ship me anywhere at any time. He also said, in an attempt inject humor, that if the army wanted me to have a wife, I would have been issued one. Two days later, a reprieve saved me. It seemed that a clerk who typed the orders was filling in for another clerk, who was on leave, and had neglected to check for volunteers to be shipped to Alaska. When this procedure was initiated, it was determined that my presence in Alaska was not required after all. My shipping orders were rescinded, and I had bit the bullet this time.

Hook Range Fort Benning, Georgia 1954

Some of the members of my committee and I were at Hook Range, preparing the range for students, who were going through the officer candidate program. We were test firing the machine guns when a buzzard flew over the range. When you are eighteen, you tend to do a lot of dumb things, and this day was no exception. I thought it might be a good idea to shoot at the buzzard. I raised the machine gun up in the air, like Burt Lancaster did in *From Here to Eternity*, and began firing. Of course, I missed the buzzard, but I did manage to set one of the other ranges on fire. Machine gun ammunition is arranged in belts with four ball rounds and then one tracer round; this allows you to keep the gun on target. The army calls this four and one. Tracer bullets are highly ignitable, and the conditions were right on this day to produce a fire. Another factor which contributed to the fire was the presence of extremely high wind.

The fire marshall and some high-ranking officers came by and questioned the warrant officer in charge, a Mister Williams. He told them that we were only firing within our range boundaries. I believe he did this to protect me, and I was, of course, grateful. The army unit will always protect its own. The fire was eventually extinguished that day, but a lot of people worked awfully hard to accomplish this.

I continued to work at Fort Benning in the daytime, like a regular civilian job, and went home at night to our duplex apartment. The only time I was separated from my new wife was when I was on guard duty or in charge of quarters.

The people in charge decided to place me in charge of the ammunition we used on our committee work. This new responsibility consisted of drawing ammunition needed for use by our committee on the machine gun range. This job made me exceedingly popular with my fellow committee members. One of my closest friends was going on leave to his home in Wisconsin, and he asked if I would supply him with some ammunition for his hunting rifle. I gave him one thousand rounds of 30 caliber machine gun ammunition, which as I have stated before was four balls and one tracer. When he returned from leave, he explained that he had a wonderful time while on leave, but he had set parts of Wisconsin on fire, just as I had done shooting at that buzzard. Fortunately, he was not blamed for the fire or both he and I would have had some explaining to do. This was theft of government property, which carried some stiff penalties. It has always amazed me to remember the wild things that I did when I was younger.

CHAPTER 15

Shipped Out to Germany in 1955

In February of 1955, I was ordered to report to Camp Kilmer in New Jersey for shipment to Germany. At this point, I had been married for only five months. A shipment overseas was the very last thing I wanted, but in the military you do as ordered. Your life is not yours anymore; you belong to Uncle Sam.

I boarded a bus headed to New Jersey for shipment overseas and Betty went to live with her sister Lily and brother-in-law Allen. We encountered some bad weather conditions on the way to New Jersey, and I arrived at Camp Kilmer one day late. As punishment, I was assigned to load the coal burning stoves in three barracks all night long. This was probably unlawful because I was a two-stripe corporal and, as such, not subject to manual labor. I did this for a couple of days before I shipped out.

While waiting for shipment overseas, a group of us went downtown in New Brunswick, New Jersey to some of the beer joints. I attempted to enter and was denied admission because I was underage. I was a corporal in the army, but was not allowed to go in and buy beer. After being turned down by several places, one of my colleagues let me borrow his card. This seemed like a good solution until I was asked his serial number, which of course I did not know. Finally, after memorizing the other soldier's serial number, we tried a different place, and they did not even check us.

We boarded a troop ship, he United States ship *Geiger*, named for some World War II hero. This began nine of the most miserable days of my life. There is something sickening about smelling saltwater in a ship rolling with the waves. It sounded like the bottom of the ship would break open. The North Atlantic is, I have been told, one of the roughest seas in the world, especially in the wintertime.

From day one, I was deathly sick from the ship rolling and the smell of vomit. The bathrooms, or heads as the Navy called them, were always consumed with vomit.

I was placed in charge of cleaning three of these heads with a crew of privates. The Navy gave me a five-gallon can of pure ammonia to clean the floor. The ammonia was supposed to be mixed with water; not knowing this, I poured the ammonia directly on the floor without mixing. It was several hours later before the head could be used. A sailor with a gas mask went in and opened a porthole. The sailor explained to his captain that some "not very wise" person had poured ammonia on the floor in full strength.

For the remainder of the trip, I was in bed with extreme seasickness. One of the sailors took pity on me and brought me a big box of saltine crackers from the mess hall. I still believe that this is what saved my life. I felt that bad.

After days and nights of misery aboard, our ship finally landed at Bremerhaven, Germany. We were at last able to feel stable ground under our feet.

They put us on a train headed for Mannheim, Germany. During this train ride, I was introduced to German beer. American beer is only 3.5 percent alcohol; with German beer, the alcohol content is 16 percent. I do not have much recollection about the train ride other than I felt rather good. This was either because of the beer or because of being on dry land at last.

In February 1955, our train approached Mannheim, Germany, and it looked as if World War II was still going on. Half of all buildings were just a pile of bricks, bridges were destroyed, ships were sunk with just one-third above the water line, and bullet holes were in everything.

The RAF (Royal Air Force) and Eighth United States Air Force did a thorough job of wrecking this city. Apparently, the people who scheduled the raids did not like something in this city.

A driver with a truck from the 2nd Armored Division loaded me and my duffel bag and transported me to Coleman barracks.

2nd Armored Division 1955

When I reported in, I found that the company commander had reviewed my 201 files, which is a record of my military history. He noticed that I was an assistant instructor on the machine gun committee, which is a part of the infantry school at Fort Benning, and he immediately offered me the job of company armorer. I was selected because of my time serving on the machine gun committee. I was considered an expert on both the 30 and 50 caliber machine guns. There were, however, a lot of other weapons that I had little knowledge of. These included the 45-caliber pistol, the 45-caliber submachine gun, the 30-caliber carbine, the Browning automatic rifle (known as the BAR), the 30-caliber M1 rifle, the 4.2 bazooka, the 60-millimeter mortar, the 4.2-inch mortar, and the 81-millimeter mortar.

Fortunately for me, the army had documented all weapons

in their manuals. I studied all these manuals until I could disassemble and reassemble all infantry weapons. The major repairs I could send to the ordnance department. I was required to conduct classes and I had to know what I was talking about.

Corporal Etheridge at Baumholder, Germany 1955

My primary job was to keep all weapons locked up and to submit a weapon report each night.

We even had a Thompson submachine gun, which was used by Chicago gangsters and squad leaders during World War II. This machine gun was only show and tell, so I was not required to disassemble it.

One of the problems with my new job was the nasty habit

the army had of placing us on alert every thirty days. This was during the Cold War with Russia, and once every thirty days, we were required to load up everything and move to the field, in preparation for war with Russia. It is fortunate that war with Russia never occurred because their tanks were three times as large as ours. There was a tremendous amount of work involved in packing up and moving out; the weapons became very dirty and our people were required to clean them. I was required to check to make sure they were clean after we returned to our barracks.

On occasion, the battalion commander, a colonel, would inspect our company. In one such inspection, he inspected the weapons in my arms room and was pleased with the clean weapons until he saw a locked cabinet. He asked me what was locked up and I told him there was nothing in the cabinet, but he insisted I unlock it. When the cabinet was unlocked, he discovered eight 22-caliber rifles which we used for target practice and were not part of the military issue. I kept these weapons locked up, so we would not have to clean them. The rifles were, of course, dirty. After the colonel left, my company commander explained to me that it was not nice to lie to the colonel. He knew I had something behind that locked door; the colonel was a very smart man or he would not have made colonel. This was one time in my life when I was very embarrassed to be caught in a lie, and I resolved to never lie again.

CHAPTER 16

Life in Germany

The 1950s were an era of live brass bands. Directly across the street from my barracks was an enlisted men's club, which played music until midnight. The problem with this entertainment was a lack of variety. They played the same songs repeatedly, so it was impossible to sleep. The one rendition I remember even to this day was "Night Train," which was a constant boom-boom-boom.

There were German workers everywhere working on our barracks. They referred to us and to each other as comrade. One of the workers carried a briefcase and I assumed he was an executive. When lunchtime arrived, he opened the briefcase, and it was filled with tall bottles of German beer, sausages, and solid rolls of bread. On every break, out would come another bottle of beer. Where I saw a lot of drunken American soldiers, I never saw a German who appeared drunk.

Germany 1955

There was what the army called a dayroom—what civilians would call a recreation room—that was next door to my arms room. The ping-pong table saw a lot of use and I played a lot. This was the area in my life where I learned to lose. I had always assumed that I was good at playing ping-pong, although not in the same category as Forrest Gump. My day of reckoning came when I played a lieutenant from Hawaii. He would put a spin on the ball that was impossible for me to return. Some parents are reluctant to allow their children to participate in contact sports, such as karate, football, and baseball. What they fail to realize is that it is important for a child to learn to lose as well as win. This was the day when I learned to lose.

In a career discussion with one of the officers about what I would do after leaving the army, I decided to attend Texas A&M University; this officer was a Texas A&M graduate. He suggested that I take a slide rule course to give me a head start at the university. The University of Maryland offered mail-in courses for active-duty military personnel. I enrolled in their slide rule course and progressed until I ran into a chapter in mathematics involving calculus. When I sent a letter to the university explaining that I had no background in this area of mathematics, the reply I received was that was unfortunate. Consequently, I was never able to finish this course.

One of the things I remember very well is their bacon and egg sandwiches, which always seemed to contain mayonnaise. I went to great lengths to explain that I did not like mayonnaise, but my complaints fell on deaf ears. It seems that the German people were obsessed with mayonnaise for some reason.

My company was conducting a live fire exercise using the Browning automatic rifle. We had about ten BARs firing, or I should say attempting to fire. The BAR fires 450 rounds per minute when operating correctly. The problem here was these BARS would only fire single shots.

My company commander observed this and called me over to tell me to try to fix it. On the way to the firing line, an old sergeant told me to check the gas ports. Our colonel drove up in his Jeep and observed all of this. I cleaned the gas ports with a wire brush and suddenly, all weapons were firing 450 rounds per minute, like they were designed for. Within a week, I was promoted to sergeant.

After my promotion to sergeant, it was decided that I had too much rank for my present job. I was sent to the second platoon as a squad leader.

This new job offered me some prestige and authority I had not had before. I now had a private bedroom that I shared with another sergeant. The army had a saying: "rank has its privilege."

Not long after my move, our platoon was ordered to the field. I believed I could handle being a squad leader but, in this exercise, I was suddenly made a platoon leader, a job for a lieutenant. The reason for this sudden action was that our lieutenant was in the hospital, the platoon sergeant was on leave, and all the other squad leaders were corporals. Since I was a sergeant, I was made the platoon leader for this exercise.

We were using armored personnel carriers, which are like tanks except they are flat on top with a ring mount designed for a 50-caliber machine gun.

Germans are fanatical about their forests, so they provide for fire breaks between trees. The problem was that to the inexperienced map reader, such as I, the fire breaks look like roads.

I instructed my driver to turn on one of these fire breaks. It soon became apparent that we were hopelessly lost, and not just my track, but the three tracks which were following me.

Very soon, two tracks were bogged down in the mud because

of recent rain. Along came the colonel, and he asked me if I knew where I was. I had to admit that I did not. The saying "up a creek without a paddle" or, in British terms, "up the brook without an oar," seemed appropriate here.

The colonel called in tank retrievers, which pulled the two tracks out of the mud. He then led me and the four tracks to our correct positions.

After returning to our barracks some four days later, I was called to the Orderly Room. The company commander informed me that, in his opinion, I was too valuable to the Arms Room, and he was sending me back. There was no mention of the incident in the field. I was secretly glad, because I enjoyed my Arms Room job.

CHAPTER 17

First Baby is Born

Betty with our first child Donna 1955

On July 13, 1955, I received a telegram from Atlanta, Georgia that said, "Daughter born well and safe, Love, Betty." There is something about becoming a father for the first time that is unlike any other emotion. I walked around in a trance for several days. We decided to name our daughter Donna Jo to acknowledge her mother's middle name. I do not know for sure where the first name Donna came from. The first thing I did was buy two boxes of King Edward Cigars and gave them out to everyone I saw or was able to stop. The cigars left in my last box I smokes myself. I need to tell Donna she was the cause of my learning to smoke.

After a new company commander was installed, I found myself back in a platoon as a squad leader and out of the Arms Room. It was decided to name our armored personnel carrier, and since we were in B Company, we had to use the letter B. In a discussion with my squad, I suggested we use the name Betty. I explained that I would not force the issue and that if anyone had another name beginning with the letter B, we would discuss it. There were no other suggestions, so we used the name Betty.

After about eighteen months listening to the boom-boom-boom, of the German live band across the street from my barracks, it was time to send me home. Orders were cut to fly me to Idlewild Airport in New York City. The airport has since been renamed John F Kennedy Airport.

I was pleased to travel by air because of the crowded conditions aboard ship and the seasickness I had endured on the way over. Our group was bused to Fort Jackson, South Carolina for discharge or reenlistment.

I was not sure after arriving at Fort Jackson how long I would be there, so I called Betty in Knoxville, Tennessee and she caught a bus to Fort Jackson. I met her and we arranged for a room at the Fort Jackson guest house.

The group of us who elected to reenlist gathered, and this was when I witnessed one of the slickest money-making opportunities I have ever seen.

There were two individuals involved: an army warrant officer who swore us in, and a master sergeant, who arranged for our reenlistment bonuses and took care of the paperwork involved. These two individuals knew all the details: how long we would be there, and how much money each of us would receive for reenlisting.

This question asked of our group was, "Do any of you need to buy a car, and would you like help finding a dealer?" Eight of our group answered yes to this question. We were all loaded into two army sedans and driven to downtown Columbia, South Carolina. When we arrived at the car dealership, I witnessed a payoff of $400 to the warrant officer. He was given $50 for each person he brought to the car lot.

I bought a 1954 Ford and drove it back to the guest house where Betty was waiting. We drove from Columbia, South Carolina to Knoxville, Tennessee where our baby girl was with her babysitters, Betty's sister Lilly and brother-in-law Allen.

When we arrived, it was late at night and baby Donna was asleep. When we awoke the next morning, Aunt Lilly brought the baby in to introduce her to her father. Lilly was holding the baby in her arms, and I remember her saying to four month-old

Donna, "This is your daddy." I held out my arms to hold her, but she immediately shook her head no and buried her head in her aunt's bosom. I realized immediately that I had been rejected. In retrospect, what could you expect of a four month-old baby who had never seen this strange man.

I decided to have a look at the car I had purchased the night before. I immediately realized that almost every window had small cracks. I took the car to an auto glass shop, and I was pleased to learn that I had purchased comprehensive insurance with my contract. The damaged windows were replaced free of cost to me.

We loaded up our baby girl and headed for Columbus, Georgia, where my new assignment awaited me at Fort Benning, Georgia.

We rented a furnished apartment and settled in. The chore of changing baby diapers was new to me, but I finally learned. Waking up at night for bottle feeding was also a new experience.

CHAPTER 18

Back at Fort Benning

I was back at the infantry school where I had served before. This time, I was to assist in training army officers. Every person on the committee was at least a staff sergeant.

My new duty assignment turned out to be the best one yet. The infantry school was closed for the holidays: all through December to January third. I was not required to go on post unless I was on charge of quarters or acting as sergeant of the guard.

When I reported in, we had our own building with Master Sergeant Black's desk and General Stillwell's office right behind. The general's father was "Vinegar" Joe Stillwell of World War II fame. He oversaw the Chinese troops as well as the American troops in Burma.

The other NCOs and I had our own special room. There were only about nine of us. Most of the sergeants were of senior rank, either sergeant first class or master sergeant. I held one of the lowest ranks on the committee.

One of my associates on the tactical committee was Master Sergeant Middleton from Texas. He was a prisoner of war, a guest of the Chinese army. We spent many hours together while on night problems. He explained that, during the Korean War, his entire battalion was captured by the Chinese due to the negligence of some of the high-ranking officers of the First Cavalry Division. He explained that all that was needed was for someone to take charge; they had trucks waiting to haul the troops to the rear away from the Chinese forces. He told me that he witnessed some of the worst behavior by the American soldiers. Some of the soldiers stole blankets off wounded soldiers while the temperature was well below zero. It was difficult working with him because he was so neurotic. I personally liked him very much. After reflecting on his experiences, I personally resolved never to become a prisoner of war.

Master Sergeant Grady, another member of our group, impressed me as a person who was preoccupied with health matters. Sergeant Grady was a World War II paratrooper who, as a member of the 11th Airborne Division, had jumped into Manilla to route the Japanese. He told some interesting stories, but like all American soldiers, some of his stories were probably true and some not. Sergeant Grady was in his late thirties and, as I stated earlier, was worried about dying. He constantly told me to make myself as comfortable as possible and to enjoy what

I had left of my life. I felt a close comradeship with Sergeant Grady because I also served with the 11th Airborne Division in basic training.

Another of my group (I will call him Joe, because I cannot remember his name), taught me something about humility. I rode to work with Joe every day. We alternated our vehicles; he would drive one week and I would drive the next. Joe was the same rank as me and we talked but he never said anything about the war. I knew he had served in Korea, but he never gave any details.

It was necessary to dress up on parade day, so we met in our room before the parade. Since I served with a lot of senior sergeants, there were a lot of people with numerous decorations. When Joe showed up with a single ribbon on his uniform, the other members were curious about his single ribbon. A ribbon represents a medal, so for every ribbon there should be a medal. When asked what the ribbon represented, he explained that it was he Distinguished Service Cross. The senior master sergeant looked it up in a book which he had in his desk. All he said was, "My goodness." I need to explain that in the American Armed Forces, the only medal higher than the Distinguished Service Cross is the Congressional Medal of Honor. Joe had never told me or anyone else that he was a war hero. He was a very humble person, and I was proud to serve with him.

Sergeant First Class Thomas Cook was another of my group who I came to know and respect. He was also another person who traded rides with me. What I remember most about Sergeant Cook was the day I closed his car door on my finger. It mashed my thumbnail so badly that I eventually lost the nail. In the 1950s, doors on Ford cars, and it was easy to slam the door on your own finger. Sergeant Cook lived on post, and I came to realize how different his German wife was from the typical American wife. His wife was an immaculate house cleaner, and she was constantly cleaning their apartment. He became a principal instructor at the infantry school, which was unique because most principal instructors were officers. The assistant instructors were all enlisted men.

I was assigned to a company inside the cartel at Fort Benning for laundry pick-up and pay purposes. One day, I drove my car inside to pick up my laundry. There was an army truck parked on one side and, when I stopped my car to go inside for my laundry, this truck blocked the road. I was only inside for a couple of minutes, and when I came out, a Major Renfro was waiting for me. He was terribly upset and told me to remove my car from the cartel and never return. He also threatened to remove my sergeant stripes but could not because he lacked authority. I immediately exited the cartel.

When I arrived at my committee headquarters, Master Sergeant Black was at his desk with the door open to General Stillwell's office. I explained to Sergeant Black that Major Renfro was very unhappy with me. General Stillwell was listening to our conversation, and he told Sergeant Black to get Major Renfro on the phone. I heard him ask Major Renfro if he thought he was God. He told the Major that he was not the Provost Marshall and lacked authority to tell me not to enter the cartel with my car. The General told me to go inside the cartel anytime I chose. I thought it prudent to avoid Major Renfro for the rest of my army career.

CHAPTER 19

Another Baby and Shipment to Korea

Betty displayed some strange eating habits in early 1956. She wanted things like pickled pig's feet and strawberries, usually in the middle of the night. Eventually she began to show signs of pregnancy, as in an enlarged belly. On September second, I took her to the hospital, assuming it was a false alarm.

I found a comfortable couch in the hospital waiting room and soon fell asleep. I had just come off a long night problem and I was exhausted.

I was awakened by a nurse, an army lieutenant. She told me that I was the father of a baby girl. In my half-awake state, I explained that we were having a boy. She laughed and told me that I was the father of a baby girl. Eventually, they let me see her, and she was the most beautiful little red-headed baby I had ever seen. We took her home and I gave out cigars. We resolved to keep trying for a boy.

In February of 1957, I was informed that I was being shipped to Korea. What followed was one of the worst duty stations in my military career. When I landed in Korea, I was back in the Stone Age: no electricity, no running water, extreme freezing weather, and temperatures well below zero.

Eventually, I was returned to the United States and sent to Fort Ord, California. In February of 1959, I received orders to return to Germany. In August of 1959, I received notice that at last I had a son. In August of 1960, I was returned to the United States and to civilian life.

When I worked at Bell Helicopter, I had a note on my desk that said, "Eventually you must shoot the Engineers and go on with production." With that thought in mind, this seems like a good time to end my recollections. I was twenty-four years old in 1960.

I would be remiss if I did not indicate my motivation or reason for writing this book. I believe it important to leave some documentation of my early life for my children, so that they can possibly benefit from some of my own mistakes or miscalculations. It is nothing short of a miracle that my offspring turned out to be the solid citizens that they are today. Not only are they so remarkable, but they all produced such remarkable grandkids for Betty and me. We could not be more pleased for the way our kids progressed through life.

I have never told them, but they all did a remarkable job of choosing their spouses. I cannot take credit for their accomplishments; they did it all on their own initiative. I refer to their education, careers, spouses, and, of course, their lifestyles.

I passionately believe that to succeed in anything it is necessary to concentrate completely in this one area and to prepare yourself beforehand by using all available resources. Whatever you do, give it all you have, but be prepared to work long and extremely hard.

Never do anything halfway and always complete what you start. Even if you fail, you will profit knowing that you at least tried. Try to have a positive outlook for the future and your dreams should come true.

Most of all, we learn from our past experiences and mistakes and must know that our Heavenly Father is merciful and forgiving and we must always put him first in our lives.

Mr. & Mrs. James Donald Etheridge

Printed in the United States
by Baker & Taylor Publisher Services